Mother of Marrow

Poetry of the Soul
by Taylor Maiden Space

Copyrighted Material

Copyright © 2009
by
Taylor Haydn Severe
All rights reserved.
No part of this book may be reproduced or transmitted
in any form or by means, electronic or mechanical,
including photocopying, recording or by any information storage
and retrieval system, without the written permission
of the Publisher, except where permitted by law.
For information address:
www.taylormaidenspace.com | www.kenosworld.com
First Printing. Printed on Acid-free paper and produced and bound in
the United States of America.
Edited by Art Severe
Artwork by Carey Thompsan, Michael Brown, Martina Hoffman,
Luke Brown and Kathryn "Ka" June.
Cover Art by Martina Hoffman.
ISBN: 0-9768518-2-2
Library of Congress Control Number: 2008940625

Acknowledgements

Thank you to Atanaha, My son, The Goddess Alchemy Project, My amazing family, super humans, SyDeFx, Hafiz, Viana Stibal, Jay Yurnell, Narayani, Aleya, Noahveil, Audette Sophia, Matthew Edwards, Lady Apples, Idiom Creak, Keno, Justice, Heidi, Koko, All of my grandmothers, Tina Malia & Sasha Rose, Peter, Evan, Egyptian djedhis, Saint Germain, hummingbirds for their heartbeats, the artists who contributed their masterpieces to this book: Kathryn "Ka" June, Carey Thompsan, Luke Brown, Michael Brown & Martina Hoffman. Thank you to Ammachi, Pleaidian wisdom, Osho, vultures, Madrone trees for their smooth branches, wild cats who refuse to be domesticated, orchids, pheasant wings, serpents of light, and to the sheer honesty of existence.

Websites for contributing artists:
www.galactivation.com (Carey Thompsan)
www.tenthousandvisions.com (Michael Brown)
www.martinahoffman.com (Martina Hoffman)
www.serpentfeathers.com (Kathryn "Ka" June)
www.spectraleyes.com (Luke Brown)

Table of Contents

Morning Revolt Against Conclusions 6
Singularity (artwork) 8
You and I Plant Planets 9
The Final Peace 11
Harmonic Concordance (artwork) 13
Turquoise Soul 14
In My Room 15
The Moon Is Full and So am I 17
Crown in Smoke 19
Caught in the Web (artwork) 20
The Unknown Lands of Woman 21
The Heroines of Voice 22
To Praise a Ghost 24
Channeling the Ashram of Tomorrow 26
Guardian of the Sky Portal (artwork) 28
Jack of Hearts 29
In Sthavara We Trust 31
Eye Wish (artwork) 34
Pure Grain 35
Rebellious Salmon Escaping the Box 38
This Belt is Tight and Suffocating 40
Travellers Handbook 41
Quetzal (artwork) 43
Your Snakey Echo Dream 44
War 46
Now is the Moment of Life 47
The Release of My Burden 48
Megaton Wonderbubble (artwork) 51
Swancat 52
Sedimenatry Backache 53
War Drinks Tea 54
Terrible Beauty 56
Melt 60
Spikes in Spine 61
Heidilove (Artwork) 62
Rubix 63
Primetime vs Timelessness 64
Paragon Space 66
November Lament 67
Myth Explosion 69
Muscles Grew 70
Me Amour Liaison 71

Table of Contents

Lotus Speech Mandala 72
Illuminations (artwork) 73
An Angel's Back 74
Jaguar Hummingbird Mantra 75
Global Warning 78
Grandmother's Seam 80
Ever Spiraling 81
Dirty Megalithic Space 82
Day of Flight 84
Seeing Through the Patterns (artwork) 85
Crossbone God 86
Collage of Fate 88
Love Poem to a Clown 89
Holy Spirit Comforter 90
God Sings in her Voice 93
Earth Crone 95
Crawling to Eden with a Smile 96
Infant Superhero 97
A Caterpillar's Reality 98
Lucid Migrant 100
S.O.S. 101
Red Window 102
Sleeping in Rhythm 103
In the Heat of Texas 104
Cerebrellation (artwork) 105
A Rare Dream 106
Airport 107
Black Crow Embryo 108
Breathe Earth Breathe 110
River Dream 111
Scribe 113
In Preparation of an Epiphany 114
Elohim 115
I Am You 116
Key 118
Cyclone Banshee 119
Diamond Soul 121
Between Breath 122
Bold Heroes 123
In This Night 125
About the Author 127

Morning Revolt Against Conclusions

My door is bolted open by antique moths that blind my seeing.
The dust of their delicate wings
carries the themes of our weaving,
paints cobalt blue healing
in between our petty hunger of needing.
This light sets stone to fire and releases the captive fury.

She is the molecular torch that guides the unseen
she is the golden thread of truth

I've read so little of the universal novel
and I crave to be taught in your temple
because fools dance with me and stroke this longing softly
into lands of fragmented symmetry.
Hope
is the circular love
that holds prayers for the children of fuchsia hues
to fractalate to.
Bear with me...
Push through...
Part the cloud's immense rapture and the thunder's terrorizing boom.
I tend to fall off mountains constructed of sacred geometry,
into palms that receive me like fruit.
Always forgiving this child for running away
into the great wide everything.
Though the deep operatic growl of eternity rattles the bones inside of she,
leaving me longing for a nothing so great and labyrinth free.
I cry to exterminate these words that bind me.

But who is this really?

Speaking,
is the red velvet caped maiden
birthing planets of white upon oceans of faces.
But truly,
the image that shatters this mirror I see,
is the beastly mother of the netherworld
who also birthed me
and crowned her human experiment kings and queens
of this great destructive everything.

solid matter accumulating and multiplying our density
dark gray ether shifting into the shape of mother.

I cry to uncrown our need to feed this modest agony.
We are children of God's masterpiece
beneath layers of free will.
So stand beside me
and revolt against the destruction of our trees
or rather
revolt against nothing.

Instead,
stand up for your soul's right to be wedded to everything.
The delicacy of a shadow's dance,
the intricate ballet of a mind's resurrection,
the moments rendered undone,
clean slate,
blank of historical conclusions
Unattached to another human
How do I do this?
This paradoxical bat cave of blinding surprise
that keeps rearranging itself to my tender eyes.
I am scattered like the limbs of Osiris,
buried at sea are the complete breaths that heal me.

No.
I am the hunter,
aiming my bow at the root of my balance,
shamanism of my own healing,
initiator of my own curiosity,
stardust in my bones,
rays of sun at my feet,
creating pathways to my own sorcery
tapestries of the collective feeling
ideas born
burnt
ash worn as bindhi

hermetic etheric beauty
deepening the souls solidity

"Singularity" by Carey Thompsan

You and I Plant Planets

In a cathartic moment of memory
I watch you summon your celestial history
your sublime home
calls you by an ancient name
her scream is deafening
she's been calling for centuries
this just in:
your mother is barely breathing

The Celestial deities solicit eternity
and beseech us to
preserve the Emerald order

to devote your cells
to your heart's honesty
with grace I bow to you and with humility
because
this is so vast
this is so deep
Judgment stone walls disintegrate into dust
blown away by holy breath
The phantom speaks
I must trust
I must trust in the muses I meet

Our original souls bend time
and paint dove wings into flight
creature of life
Your eye is my vision quest
My body your meadow
I merge into your divine earthquake of hot tears
And pull back my lost mind
To this eternal harvest of ripe
Unswallowed by the hunger
Unbound by the puppet's rope
Under your gold seat
Where you hide the pharaoh's secret
Beneath your soul's feet
Is where you keep it
While gazing the giant galaxy

with my unfurled eyebrows
We witness beings like you and I
in the dense galaxy of our minds

This nation of the image
that holds our beauty captive
longs with tranquil essence
to be free
This auric frequency of consciousness
awaiting entry
into this gate we call Earth
of hidden majesty
A reality where language is futuristic telepathy
and feathers make fallen angels quiver endlessly

We sit alongside gold cuffed epiphanies
awaiting the great nothing
to dispose of our rubbish entirely
a life beating pulse in this very moment
where the tribe and the light of being
fuse as one flame in the tilted eye of our seeing

The dream of a double headed serpent
slithers into formation of a mockingbird
and we pause time
to sink into our breath again.

What meditates beyond the Skin?
What bends us beyond space?

when we reach out our infant palms
into the ancient unraveling
to peal away the barbed wire of separation
we find this seed
calmly awaiting our presence
singing a familiar lullaby
we seem to know at birth
extending a hand to dance with
between the original cracks of time
This
is the dense galaxy
that makes up you and I.

The Final Peace

The past identity I once knew as me
Has crumbled into dust rocks of epiphany
Melting in liberation off my fingertips
As I laugh in unison with these cathartic Earthquakes

Praying at night for the plants to breathe life
As the pink child of God dances in delight
This union sets ancient moths free tonight.

Ages have passed
That I have wept awake in carnaged rooms
Searching for citrine
To call my master
because
Patterns of sacred scribes have been stolen
Hearts of grace have been nearly broken
Maps to the diamond have been demonically hidden
Necks have been bitten

Finally,
the sweet sound of the soul's song
Is completely guiding me.

The holy lotus is perched on a planet birthed by blue whales
Swinging holy feet
In the ocean that is her pond
Receiving a slight vibration of sacred essence.

In tone I am cradled
By her gold petaled
Soul drenched offerings of forgiveness

In the remembrance of love
we are bridged back to the celestial temple
The eternal space that houses our souls
The impenetrable shrine of compassion
That bathes us in beauty as we repent
The ever fluid opera of angels
The state of dream we long not to wake from

Though

Sometimes
Through wounded eyes
The Earth is a withering shack being devoured by termites

But palm leaves
Invoke jaguar eyes to pierce through the need
As the coral crested goddess
Traces the light of our planted seeds

And offers her soul to our hearts that bleed

This miracle of birth is possible
This thought
That the ascension of our souls is beckoning
Is the only thing left that feeds me
Unity
Peace
In all of its entirety

hermetic etheric beauty
deepening the soul's solidity.

"Harmonic Concordance" by Carey Thompsan

Turquoise Soul

My soul moves into you
a new cell grows
languid symbiosis
merging color and form.

Mine is a lyrical soul dance
a fire I yearn to keep burning
casting images into our sky
for the crying angels to gaze into.

I wish to participate
in re-writing our future's history
to facilitate in teaching the broken
how to dance again
showing the statues how to cry from infinity's lullaby
I wish to clasp the hands of my energy body in constant
prayer for love's revival
to leave room in my mind for all to transform
to sweep the floor of the home in my heart
so that you may sleep
upon the bearskin of my soul
with the turquoise stones of Earth
I paint this image whole.

In My Room

Levitating in mute air
and stopping my world from moving
altars warp themselves around me
to calm my breathing
I am feline
circling the Sphinx
I am the backbone of endangered fish
caught in nets
drunk by the depth of the sea
this incarnation has sculpted me invisible
and physical.

I die, each breath to be born new
in repentance
evacuating broken stitches that held together
my hidden secrets
when my eyes turn towards crystal remembrance
archaic essence ignites birth within me
when i gaze into this creation,
quietly consumed by it that is mystery
I wonder,
what is the ultimate curiosity?
Is it of origin of form?
Or the history of thought?
I have been told
that
beyond the blackness of space
is a halo of colors
announcing an ancient crone queen of loving
delivering us from our suffering

In between breaths of paused time
her creation into our moments halt the chaos of existence

when each moment is approached with respect
I am dissolved of questions
I seek color vibrancy
shooting from the invisible beginning

because there is no end worth grieving
skies move beyond miles high
and the sight ceases what we grasp as reality
ascending us beyond our world
alleviating our primordial tears

I am returning to my root
to find the seeds that sprouted me
hand woven blankets cover my shivering journey
as the ice melts to a tender warmth
i see flowers become the eyes
that see us beyond our global disguise
we dangle in space
you and I
The song of bounty blinds the sight
when we stop looking
we see.
When we see
We find the voice that has been whispering to us ineffably

I trace the figure 8 on my forehead to see.

The Moon Is Full and So am I

This evening
Is full with the tender white tears of weeping clouds
Once firm dams are rupturing
Unleashing the Ganges River at our feet
Woman
swollen with everything.

Swallowed by the underground black hole of the Universe
delicate heart murmurs sound like waves to me
Beneath burning skin
the marrow of my bones calls to Mother Mary
she cloaks me in her red cape
where a fetal heartache for Earth is soothed
I drink her suffering to spit the poison into Gods fire
transmuting the dark ionic embers
when the elixir of gloom touches my lips
I weave this tattered garment
with the gold in my soul
to summon solidity
to mimic the gates of heaven
to steep with humanity in the broth of source.

Man is often too much man for me

too fixed and condensed

I cleanse the birth pains of Earth through my womb
I purge the violence of humanity through my breath
Man is solid as gate for me to pass beneath
thick as Redwood
dense as lava
He anchors my dismantled floating soul
which shifts form through electric currents
and magnifies exploding entities

Do not disturb man at work

I am woman of mortal elixir
untamable star fire for blood

bloody
woven with the well water only dragons drink from
braided to my ancestral DNA
composed of every thought I have ever had
Man: earth stone, jade staff
penetrating gaze full with words and conclusions
I am loved by you for being a flame
a home to sink your silence into
I sing lullabies to disincarnate souls hiding in the emotions of people
I am woman of secret meaning
Underlying tones of vortexual feeling
I am your birth
keeper of the microcosmic galaxies in your body
I am titled eyes of silence
witness to illusion
prayer upon tongue holding dead child
resurrecting Earth
Man: holder of keys
keeper of meaning
Map maker of my overflowing star infused sight
stoic straight spine
pulling light into soil
Man cradles infancy
warming icebergs with sun palms
with calloused feet
Man carries woman over sharp diamond shards of debris
but she grows wings and claws to match
clenching necks into space
Man learns of silent wisdom
given freely upon invisible altars
woman awakens to what she gives
dances translucent dance of serpentine code
Man is 3-D bridge builder
but I am levitating in ether
above ground
disintegrating into light
Man knows talk and form and wires and strength
and I am cave woman with candle
weaving mudras with light
I am soft skinned and cloaked
gazing into source imploding eyes
My body is Hathor's landscape.

Crown in Smoke

As I pray ruthlessly
to a gold plated mind shaped
fractalated epiphany
the witness becomes me
engraving scars of remembrance
into my skin as surrender
Where there is love
There is life
and intercommunication with your God of choice
I am unraveling the labyrinth rug that shapes me into curious form
desperate to shed scales
I am burning this home
for wings
praising the ebb and flow of serenity
shaving my moon scented cranium
philosophy
to merge deep
alone I am today beneath brilliant natural light
invigorating the wept cells within my main frame
If we are to GO
into this shape-shifting moment
we conclude so foolishly within
Let us do so semi-mindlessly
with our hearts in the cups of our palms
Or sculpted mysteriously by the highest maker we can invent of ourselves
Let us meet inside of the golden flame
that forms into rivers
flowing with the notes of our Grandmother's song
You are an ancient symbol carved into my heart
I beat steadily to your corn maze dance
I move like serpent to your flute
Watching crowns disintegrate into holy light particles
before that dense tubular operatic choir of angels
we dream of each night as feeling.

"Caught in the Web" by Martina Hoffman

The Unknown Lands of Woman

Sleeping in Rhythm
in this bedroom
my fingertips paint the opaque walls bright
and the vital needs of my inner song to be sung
is as alive
as the porcelain doll
in a little girls mind
I am observing the shadow of candle light dreams
soaring into you
then soaring into me
It is of a cryptic code That I did break
while gazing into the cast eyes of our eternity
I did not fade Away into this tender and poetic day
I have embodied the doll of boundless energy
by frequenting the thoughts of exquisite beauty
beside every crevice of fractal fertility
I am seen by your dream
I am shattered by its scream
I am lost in a paradise of bliss

as I claw into your delicate back again

the thorn in my side
that allowed me to hide
has softened to a round gem
it is glowing in the face of our freedom
and singing of a forgotten song to mend

this is the band of the flying phoenix

released from the quickening sand
spread open at last
glowing in the gaps
between the known and unknown lands of woman.

The Heroines of Voice

I'm not sure if we are divine evolution
or Darwin's nightmare
but
beneath the heat of the quiet mind
that resurrects our black and blue eyed crime
the human displaces itself
and sits empty
on a wool rug
meanwhile
I glide on the swan's black wings
those unstable wings
made of jigsaw
and dry ice dreams
elixirs trailing the tears in my eyes
shed in blazing light

awakened and heard are my cries
embedded as flowers in our children's minds
awakened and heard are my cries

this earth is perfect
she rotates in faith
because the drunken
and the insane
still sing in the rain
even as the hail savagely taunts their name

the darkness begs to be light
it too craves love
it too needs sight

I know the spirit can hear our benediction
in its silence
or in its screams
the naked
and the astray
and the karmic chisel that sculpts their days
we've shaved the lions mane
and then prayed
before his golden sight
dancing like dervish mad children
afraid of what we'd done
beneath a watching moon's light

in order to sink into this
i ask for the madrone branch
to wrap me in trance
and grow cactus pricks
to initiate my lips
i bow to the ladder that never ends
with blood laced kisses
its steps leading to man's repentance
For me
to resonate with this
i need for the Earth to drink me
I crave for her to invent me

she, this being
I am her daughter
her son
her fetal creation
we are made of her essence

to paint this life
with the brushes of beauty
to resurrect deep epiphany
we must walk
in the land of our spirits proclivity
we must surrender our cowardly guns
that pierce through time with fear
we must assassinate hate with grace
to rejuvenate the jewels in this place
steady our feet to a poised mudra
unaffected by city streets
love etch a sketched in the eyes

we are the heroines of voice
weapons of mass laughter
armies of beauty
on the front line
burning the collective scorn
bringing images
so profound
that the war itself weeps
awaking the people
from this dense
impossible sleep
we are the heroines of voice
the keepers of keys
the lovers of joy
the bringers of peace.

To Praise A Ghost

I am the fool
awaiting contact from priestess embrace
so silent am i
in her decadent wake
even spellbound
speechless
founded and tamed by her full moon smile
i am a child

and she is the goddess that has no logic
no name
she is crazy and grace
merged to mad

rounded not squared
she is the eye of the storm
fallen to pieces
like crumbled leaves upon dying trees
perpetuated my knot so that i could see
turned me from the inside out
placing words of beauty in my mouth

she tears a droughtful day for Earth
in chamomile water as i pray
leaving me bricks of gold
to rebuild my home

of course she was wrapped in a white procession
and protected by chariots of love
embroidered blankets
and wings of dove

even in the still wind night
where i paint myself into the sky
where her scent still is worn on my skin essential
even in this night
still as statues wind
where I've loved my rival
and worn my tattered dress

we paint together this mural in our dreams
where she is the mother of what is free
the ever-changing paint
morphing the face
perfecting the taste
that pours into my mouth
and softens my grip

and when she looks at me
as to say "stay"
even though she birthed me with wings
even though she weeps to hear me sing
that tangerine lullaby we weave
her voice echoing
growing warm in the winter's cold infirmary
the blanket of we unravels entirely
leaving the she
and the she that is me
to awaken from sleep
to be.

Channeling the Ashram of Tomorrow

Caressing the nape of your spruce scented neck
to explore the contours of your shape
I sing asteroids of erupting fire upon your cheek
in this blue flame sheepskin night

our eyes catch glances
in the space between our mirrored chances
like this liquid of ivory rain
that pours out of my dripping fingertips
as though emerging from the sky's eternal lake
while in commune with the nameless face
fallen upon the slanted slopes of today
I seek space
in silence and prayer
hands glued
like a steeple's point
clasped
to form a child's dreamland

landscape of the mind
unoccupied
green and plasmic

washed to land
in a bottle made of dissolving sand
is this planet's exit plan

she crawls into our very spines
spreading to the nucleus of our vacant eyes
giving flight to our souls on standby

to enliven our sight
writing the poetry of our campfire songs
in this endless night

caressing the nape of your spruce scented neck

i think of this web we weave
and this blue pearl
her melting ice
flooding our desert pilgrimage

lift us above the trash and the tangle
to crawl inside of your ancient face for a moment

with your piercing opalesque fiery sight
and the depth of a thousand unleashed minds

as the cracks of this world parts supremely
this unraveling calls
to our nameless names
and spirals us
suddenly
into spacious space
OH
to be face to face
with this immensity
to give birth to this angel of death
to be merged with this infancy
let us melt beneath this creativity
let us truly claim joy as free.

"Guardians of the Sky Portal" by Carey Thompsan

Jack of Hearts

Your wholeness is evidence of angels breath
burrowed as poetry inside of God's perception
we dream reality into being
requesting light to caress the darkness
we offer our vessels to the eternal heartbeat
taming the wild winds with this lucid breath

Sometimes the pain is a catalyst for motion
where the cells lay dormant
life inflates its essence into being

the crystal quartz crone is here to summon our depth of beauty
to build bridges out of rose stems that we may levitate above

our lovers speak the languages of the soul
inviting the molecules of light
and the density of matter
to unify
to reflect each other entirely
to thank each other for being

The mother knows us as child
and helps us to master what we have already learned

Reminding us to dance
with the rhythm of the heart
to activate lost mandalas
to decode irretrievable archives
of crucial memory

to excavate mystery
the essence of a brave God's dream
loves us into being
birthing queens as stars

even through the thin veil of tar
the dismal old paradigms dangle
light prevails in its graceful explosions of thought

In this dream
density evaporates into ether
and beckons the sweet inhalations
we find God within

Beside the glimmer of the moths dusty wings
the Universe awoke in me
became my chaperone
into this myriad mystery
expanding the vastness of our tribe's mythology

Angel, be real
reveal yourself
as woven to the raw oracle of space
reveal your vulnerable tears
to the Vulcan that sleeps lucid in your sight
becoming steadfast supernova
imploding into the depth of deep skies
let us see each other
to fix gaze with the opal iambic eyes
bearing banners of truth upon lips
to oscillate in tandem to the Earths heartbeat

Light obliterates dark

and ignites evolution in a most poetic way
it does not ever dull itself on its own
only in the shade of darkness does it seem to vanish

but it has not.

have faith in its strength

to walk beside the Syrian King
while de-masking his infancy

he is in service to our innocence
impeccable warrior eyes
saves lives

and humbly asks for love

In Sthavara We Trust

My voice is comprised of nameless moments
that I have only in this one become aware of
Auspicious notes
in handled journals
worthy of diagrams and collaged offerings
This maniacal breath of man that breathes sulphur upon necks
withers rose colored vision into yellow asylums
I step forth to the altars of holy children
to ressurect their comatose mothers
with cathartic jubilance
awakening sleeping beauty illusions
Delicate minds lay awake with celestial eyes
widened to the obscurity of man
weaving leaking wounds
with the violet perfume
of white hearted mantras
for the purpose of re-generation
warrior minds step forth
into the flooded adobe homes of your souls
to drain the built up tears of your withering.

With or without you, this ascension is igniting
When the wind woven guardians of our evolution step forth
to guide us to that cliff
that cliff we sweat in our dreams within
wings will emerge suddenly
not before flight
but only after leaping abruptly with bare backs
wings of golden merkaba light
held by vapors of angelic breath

this is faith
this is the degree of trust in our souls we must aspire to
to truly know the intricacy
of this stone etched novel we call life
I, like you, am a vessel
a conduit
for the eagle to soar out of me into open hearts that bleed
I am the bee's pollen
drank of to infuse birth into bellies blooming with Earth Microcosmically
designed to represent the divine
Like you,
lotus petals fall from the garden in my heart
when thoughts of hate cut the air around me
Like you,
I am composed of Gods molecular brilliance
braided to the archangels angular shadow
Like you,
I am orchestrating the symphony of my own unique existence,
fulfilling contracts with the higher realms that beckon me,
I have been resonating in this brilliant body of disintigrating clay since Egyptian
hieroglyphs lined my bedroom wall,
since Sirian starships scoped my brain waves from afar
and delivered me into my mothers 3-D womb of gravity
I, like you,
am incarnate in form again
slightly seduced by this perpetual state of shock
catapulted into spirals of dervish shaped mind scapes struck by the
lightning of beauty
and awakened each moment by my first infant breath
recalling burning temples in my vine embedded dreams
like you,

I am witnessed by the unseen
Following my mother
into harmonic realms of wyverns and silent communication
With humble fingertips
we pull
upon the white shards of crystalline light
to merge
with the Earth's weeping ecosphere of life
This is the prayer of an illuminated servant of Earth
This is the path home
that our furthest chambers of feeling long to walk
The true collective voice of Earth is sounding.

In Sthavara we trust.

"Eye Wish" by Kathryn "Ka" June

Pure Grain

2000 angels
released from the prison of their parents
move into the homeless spaces of the sun
touching upon the basic occupation of cellular souls
eating acid
curling time
unfurling paradigms
sugarcube games bounce upon Kevin's white walls
casting us into an elaborate game of paper cut out acting
looking into eyes

"Do you know what's about to happen?"

daisy Bombs drop upon the slits of open eyes
stepping into new spheres of crazy observation
outside the normalcy of now
where beauty walks into one's new crystalline sight
people chase the visuals in my head
but I am protected by the magnetism of friendly LSD
liberty
freedom in running upon Harlem Avenues silent abyss
twilight tinges
stopping thoughts
unifying color
red changes all knowing
when police dogs run into empty spheres
with blank sirens
and unanswerable questions
I run
across lanes and dimensions
in the shapes of medians
angling cubicle intersections
dream police circle angels
harvesting the seeds of their futures
but I am true to my Western self
upon route 30

where my soul is found
California feeds visions of tan Lamborghinis
and Hawaiian white melodies
the story of an unaware woman
satisfied with emptiness
through my past I explode sound memories
a floating blur shooting lightning with force
void of mass
I gather information to catapult into the core of Earth
protected by iron awareness
and true awakening
galactic shape curls into all crusts of experience

I am molecular form

becoming sediments of Earth
like different forms of life
beyond interpretation
the brightness of light beckons me to the ocean's life
through millions of years of looking at myself from behind
morphing into the future human of my vision
I ride a majestical horse of light
sitting like a regal dark landscape
beneath no ozone layer

we are outer space on Earth

A most vivid retreat coils one into safety
alone
untouched

Meanwhile
In past dreams
I dig into the screams of asphalt
hogtied
and peeled from my mother
disturbed
I see morbid intention of law
darkening the light
bending angels over backwards for the devil to fuck
I am thrown behind the closed doors of hate
driven to hell

my reflection witnessed
in the puddle of my sweat
keys hidden
incoherent masked mind playing quiet abuse
a monster grabs an angel's jaw
popping holy awareness from wet saliva
jumping with hunger
to salvage the droplets of consciousness
I am transported from inner space
to other worldly realms
"Are you okay?"
asks the ghost of fear
"Are YOU okay?"
asks the portal of light
the light penetrates through mulching tar
that pokes and prods vitality into disbelief
observing voices of friends

salvation sees you

Laughs at you

reminds you of eyes
awake to God and the nameless faces

I see you

tattooed warlock of apprehended light
igniting nightmares of catheter fixed pain
visuals sustain celestial sight
I ask the little man of silent knowledge
how to be free
relax
cooperate

be released to your mother

but my mother doesn't want to know my secrets

Rebellious Salmon Escaping the Box

You are the rebellious salmon upstream
alone against the tide of petrified shock
the un-walked caves within you talk
using language more like colors than words
I heard them tiptoeing with mine
in the beauty sphere at the end of time
while singing to shadows
and tumbling through space
i saw the shifting grace of people in your face

We come from a sphere
that changes shape each moment
with our hand made wings of labradorite shine
pieces of puzzled minds
to piece together and find
that the mountains we imagine ourselves as
crumble in time

I wake up in the rubble
my hand is holding my lip
my Eyes wide and tender
my skin has turned to leaf
my fingers long and slender

like this cataclysmic shatter of thought
the fish break out of their school of knots
pseudo teachers
teaching the children how to pronounce their own names
compounding the heart
throwing kerosene to the flame of mind games
pseudo teachers
wandering in an empty landscape
denying the green
and the waves
and the warmth
sharks with great tall teeth
purple and hypnotized
striped with leopard skin gills
hunting in thirst for fish

call out
but receive no cry

for the slithering amphibious primordial kin
has escaped into the decadent beauty of this moment

there is no xerox copied eye gazes
in the stone stoic sight of a gypsy

there is no pre-meditated broken thought
to lay shattered in his home
there is no fungal funk of dismay in his trunk overgrown
there is a pouring spout of organic broccoli sprouts
expelling out of his ether
he is not toad stuck in mud
or unicorn fable
he is frankincense and myrrh
and the blank page that begs you to pour unto
he is thick winter coat fur
he is not sir
or punk
or slime
he is divine banshee wine
and he tastes like lightning lime
this is what happens kids
fish
Gods
when you escape the terrain of the cubed matrix

the thoughts turn to friend
and the heart to lover
the baby is born again
and the texture of your unique scent
makes people to quiver.

This Belt is Tight and Suffocating

This belt is tight and suffocating
this moment is a poisonous snake
dancing
a concerto of lessons beating me into oblivion
until I disappear so much I become light
grounded into the soil
hooked into steel
this breath is my victory
when it is slow
and deep
contorting memories
all dimensions
align in unity

this immensity actually does unravel me

and I become suddenly too aware of gravity
and you are the beast that has slain me
the same is for me
your face is shaved for me to sleep still upon
but I can never cuddle with fire
that is certain in waves I ride upon
my back aches when wings grow
your face and its curves blend with me
aroused to touch your human form
with my soul's poetry
but you are busy
the lotus is sitting on me
and my pen is scribbling esoteric obscenities
that liberate my suffering
yesterday,
when you had respect for me
I was the branch of an ayahuaska tree
Today
I am a pink martini
poisoning.

Travellers Handbook

search no more
you already are the self
channeled into the soothing ashram of no-time
missing fences un-gate the mind
un-cuff your labyrinth search to be free...
you already are
you see?
it is as simple as turning around
you don't have to wait to be found
the imitated whisper
carried into the vast garden of God
is a facade
I am shaken awake by this atrocity
I am reopened
put together again in musical grace
I am encapsulated by the prayer
In my palm's secret eyes
as the bottom of the island's crystal floor
invites me in to cry
my eyes paint warm embrace
to those floating upon the lotus face
there is indeed
a paved road of giants
and a stratospheric thought of maze
though I am distant in my cave
listening to the spiraled face
speak of delicate chances
mirroring my feeling
catching her glances
this is the thunder's boom
tacitly unable to speak
lacking in ego meat
she is rather meek
beside spirit's wordless song
a path of flowers she walks upon
quantumly train wrecked into divinity
to be myself
to avoid decay
I contain thyself

as slowly as the muse may lay herself
upon your bed of rose scented sheets
within your garden of beats
forms of your beauty bury themselves
beneath your condition of hate
detach from detachment itself
only grace can release the waste
the heart responds only to the angel's face
only to the inherent happiness
of consciousness itself

Therefore

in humble homes
to be witness
is to be
the vibrating bliss of consciousness
and to feel the inquiry of innocence
is to be the risen avatar
the dove colored goddess
the first feeling of existence
the eye blinding light they call star
strategically placed
and prayerfully blessed
awakened by play
and love
into oneself deeply
in nature's true formation
alive to feel again
this is no sin
though
this knowing has defeated the devil
again
and again.

"Quetzal Knowsleep" by Kathryn "Ka" June

Your Snakey Echo Dream

my eyes are melting
a burning castle
to hot sand
as i penetrate myself in the wake of you
surrounded vastly by the sky's oceanic girth
This ego is crowned last standing
in the desert oasis of me,
sun-burned my cool skin,
turning fate from scales to feather
if i should curl myself so deeply within
that i wind outward to you again
and if i should be unable to hide my eyes
tilted green with tears
perhaps you could build a toy boat
to catch my rain within
offer it in your hand
to the dried vegetation
thirsty for passion
i shake like a rhythmic earthquake in glass skin
to shatter
entirely
without even seeking the pieces
to be built new,
my daily birth,
like this unread novel i wrote in trance
I burrow inside of this pure existence
sleeping in the soil of its precious voice
coiled eternally like the DNA of angels
and the ragged teeth that ate me free
I've severed them
and wear them jeweled around my neck
as prize
as memory
as religion

To watch you in your sleep
and to imagine the layers of your dreams
one day will be the cataclysm of this friction
magnetically pulling my heart to you
shaking away the iron walls of our distance
while drinking the nectar of truth

I'd speak some form of invented French
in my cave dwelling mind with you
refusing the broken seams of muffled screams
bowing to the silence before the machine
my lord could be a 7 winged beast of prey
that stalks my wickedness
recycles my shadow to feed me light
by way of ragged teeth and a wand

War

This is the end of the eternal triumph of war
the veterans of your greed
are hanging on the cross we collectively carry
Our backs ache with your burden
whoever you are
the condensed demon of laziness
or the symbol of our subconscious massacre
Occasionally,
I cry as though every deep withered well of tears
has overflown within my soul
This is the end of the eternal triumph of war

Now is the Moment of Life

The sound lives in the base of my spine
where serpents practice geometry
carving their history into my back
fire escapes from my grasp
and ignites a fury of sacrifice upon a lamb

how soft this future is
warm child with perfect palms
and eyes of ice that melt

these words seem too much like words to me

too much like words

The Release of my Burden

In Sanskrit camouflage
I hid beneath your sight,
in-between time
on the darkest night.
It was the linguistic masquerade
to the deep caves of modern poetry,
recorded by the soul's heart
and a face of feathers scarred,
prayers in form of breath,
eye to eye with death.

This moment is very real.
It is from hyperspace reality,
more profound than gravity
outlined in gold spotted caress
cascaded through infinity
uncaught by the net.

I've un-spoke this language,
carried away by time and space,
adjacent underground to the eyes on your face
planted like wilted stems in the forest reaching for air
In the deserts hot throat
where I found my telescope
and spotted you.
Where I saw no cackling witch
or escaped monsters I could not tame.
Recycled my glass
Played some game
Was witnessed by the peering hawk eyes of prey
Fell unto my knees when I learned to pray.
Love... I used to call to you like you were a distant star,
when the simple now of love seemed too far.
Night full sky dream man
You are the holiest he!
beneath the heart cabins that protect me,
a spiraled fire I found in thee!

Tree covered leaves
awoke in honesty
and knelt down beside me.
We've unraveled this knot of history
by the divine will of the wandering gypsy.
Free
is she
and he
and we
We are the eyes that weep of prophecy!
Disguised in mask to conquer the burden
we rise at last to feed the serpent...
coiled around this tree of antiquity
perception shattered in its spy like victory
A body that's lead by the mind's leash
stands quivering before this grand tree.
If I could write this forever
I may enjoy Eternity!
Webbed like spider fingers in the lair of your echo,
I've even learned to play piano.
So,
Shian your warrior
and unleash your storm
crawl into your silence
become true form
this is my dream
this is how I pray
this is what soothes my labyrinth days.
You are the pale white light beyond me,
the mountain beside my river
the faint whisper in the shape of swan
the full spectrum of an ancient song...
How can I stop thinking of he?
when this spiral has become we?

So I am falling with grace
to kneel beside surrender
in the delicate twist of a genius mind bender,
pouring the light in the eyes of my palms

to vertically grasp the mother's arms.
In the beginning,
you are the altar
and after prayer
you are the key
In the middle
you are the story
written by the lines in-between
You are the mountain
the river
the sky
and the dream....
I am writing this with my left eye
unafraid of anything
unraveling
unraveling

"Megaton Wonderbubble" by Kathryn "Ka" June

Swancat

A fair feathered cat
covered in language
flew itself into the corner of my universe
and directed the traffic of my thoughts
recalling river dreams
by the flow of my now nicely flowing frequency
she channeled amethyst history
that instantly revived my being
with lotus shaped petal paws
and gardenia scented breath
she swam into my memories
and chanted love songs into my death
the metallic eons of cyclical fear
dispersed before her opera
of which the stars sung to her
when she was a moonbeam's daughter

Sedimentary Backache

In dark indigo nights
flushed pale by emotion
charcoal resides in the hand of a child
smudged face,
unfinished painting
picture framed on Mama's wall

There is no room to grow in a box
all tangled in fish hooks and rain
caught
by a God's creation am I
I grow just as a planet might
sun and water rubbed into me
I am just behind a door
I even see its opening
though this vision blurs
these eyes cannot see through its fog
The music paints the dots for me
I am so empty
ressurect me!!
comfort this need burrowed into me
that seeds itself
opens my wounds
and bleeds itself
I don't fall to pieces
I turn stoic stone neutral statue
I need about 30 days alone with the sweet succulent dirt
so that I may be an appetizer for God
so that we may again dance
with the hips of cobra
those untamable
always shocking gyrations of ecstacy I so miss

I fear I may grow mold upon my sedimentary back among this.

War Drinks Tea

war surrenders
and what is left
is the reflection of yourself
layered in stain glass perfection

before this phenomenon
i am poet to you
i am the weaver of proclamations
naked
draped only in the sound of words

to him
i am partner
lover of every curve
witness to every subtle movement in the stream of our river
to him
i am home
mother to his tiny child
listener to his heartbeat
to me
he is the castle walls
he is the breath that stokes the fire
that heats
he is the waterfall
i can barely breathe within
but within him
breath is transcended

to spirit
we are the alchemical future
cloaked in the moths dusty wings

to me
i am an undeniable banshee singing
i am human in-between
my skin is soft and warm as a mother pheasant's wing

i have a mind
my heart bleeds
I am tiny seed
i am a hurricane
my body is a temporary dwelling
i foolishly identify with

to me
you are pillar
I serve the tea at your lament
in your eyes is where hyenas relax their hunger
you are the fuel to the angels epiphany
you are existence expressed honestly

i wear my heartbeat on your ring.

Terrible Beauty

In this empty book of us
that you write unintelligible tongue upon
mazes lay spiders into my brain
and send shivers to my spine

You
holy fool
who paints murals in my heart
with crimson blood brush strokes
and 16 different names

You
untamable
ivory bald headed beast
leaping like an anvil upon my fragility

shooting bullets through my open palm
with your jade pistol weapon
I so longed for

I made elixirs
to heal the broken souls of your feet
while coiled in fetal lament beneath them

I swam in the pristine waters of your essence
drowning the deep end of your soul

I carved a hole in my heart as a bed for you

I found my way through your maze to meet you

I loved you

between cellular breakdowns
and
blank jigsaw puzzled K-holes

my cells exploded into life
as I would float weightless
into divine epiphany

Would you believe
i've slept with earplugs
in hell's master bedroom
trying to go blind
as not to fear you

because that sudden knowing of truth
would beckon the Goddess in me
and that would set my divinity free

and if I were to hear the bronze bell of awakening
I would have to burn my whole mansion

would you believe
I've been pushed off cliffs
for not matching
the delicacy of an orchid

bitten by poisoned doves
for carrying scrolls of freedom

this is the netherworld
I curled within
to worship your golden body

your essence was so rare
and so corrupted
I tried to catch my tears in a tulip's petal
so that I may stitch
my last thread of life
to my soul

secretly praying to grow gardens
of liberty inside of me

bound and silent
with ulcers and screams

I tried to be your impossible queen

perhaps I could be
sculpted with a white glowing perfection
cave driven into prophetic wisdom

I believed
that if enough eyes
of the tender child
were to merge with snow capped daggers

You might just love me

I remember you making love to me at midnight
in that river
holding me
with the hands of a soft prince
and the jade staff of a beast

To the skies you declared me as your wife

I accepted
if you promised
to release me of mechanical death
and brush my hair
and lick my sweat

but as I whispered this to the world above
I hid in cloaks
from a most relentless thirst
that crippled my throat
and left me to burst

I starved the holy spirit in my heart
with fingers to my spleen
and my mother's absent voice

but I loved you

you captivated my voice ineffable
and in this searching for sound
to express my passion for you
I found God chanting celestial mantras
into my bones

In this desperate search into the netherworld to find you
I found the lighthouse of my soul in your place

So for this,
I thank you.

goodbye
to the deep cave salt water explosions of agony
I release you to the guardians of infinity
that you may be transmuted
to light the dark forests of the soul
and intertwine
with the blissful essence of being.

Melt

i reach for your hand and it melts
the wick you have grown inside of you
is flammable to my fire
eyebrows raise
eyes tilt
space invades me
melding my flesh into its delicacy
into the flavors that live so deep
no human can taste
my feet are petrified to the structure of tree
rooted into the rich soil that has created me
this is the moment where my pale complexion
turns indigo blue
where the footsteps that were you sink into

I am Indian mother
beaded with tradition
holes in my spirit's heart
from iron bullets
disguised as butterflies
taste of salt on my tongue
tobacco in my lungs
to no one i belong
i am particles of quartz freedom
embedded amethyst old growth into wounds
licked clean by the highest library of dreams
I am impenetrable bronze statue
with roses for feet
vibrating with the echo of eternity
warmed by the wings of a phoenix
and his fire that comforts me
to activate the harmony
that sleep rewards me
I pledge my allegience
to the woven web of this pen's divinity.

Spikes in Spine

Coarse moment grows like spikes upon my stegosaurus back
turns me inside out
and shivers the warmth to hot
and the cool to cold.
I know that beyond my magnified eye of you
there is indeed a ripe soft fruit that never spoils.
I feather the back of your hand lovingly
as mother
as child
as saint
remembering your eyes
and the seed you sprouted in me
when I watched you take flight to she
There are no ropes around your ankles
the red scars upon your neck
seem to be made by the watery stems of change
delicately woven together
by the hands of a small child
Let the pieces of jigsaw puzzle pain
uproot from our backs
to fall back to the earth of which it came
Into the hearts of those eyes that lost us
to heal their layered minds in the fire's maze.

"Heidilove" by Kathryn "Ka" June

Rubix

I dissolve before all constructions of the rubix mind
And gather my particles
upon the blue lotus that my mother holds.
When I am no longer bound
to the secret screaming of patriarchy
that has chanted its mantras of history
into wandering child shaped ears, I live.

Prime Time vs. Timelessness

I was right in the middle of killing the toxic scream that haunts me
It was the assassination of my woes upon this season of cold marble tile
with black and white pin-striped eyes and the sea's orange shrine
remembering the flood that almost washed away this child within me that plays
feathers laughing at beautiful blue jean black girls,
still alive
still spectacular
as she was crossed by the crowd's cackling keys
locked from sight of freedom
liquid pulse
a wordless vacancy upon a bluish backdrop
she turns away into her poetry
to wash away the persistent stains of society
bolts of lightning lay sideways in her wake
while names are reborn to her taste
down beside the water's wet starship
unafraid of believing
while pretend policemen unroll their red carpets to watch
men sipping out of the female's hour glass
smirking with a clown's feeling
and hands firmly pressed to heart
outside the gates of Purple Mountain's Majesty
the black woman is unable to speak
worlds carried over her shoulder like a couch to run home to
She is lotus on a bamboo carpet
un-eaten by city lights
on their tails in fact
climbing backwards to the ancient mortar,
compiling words of wishes in her mind
as though preparing to encounter God
(the elder Olympian who grew too fast to run)
but I remember turning
to kiss your Mohawk tongue
made in Mexico with love
songs of tango sung
and parts of my heart strung

I learned to see who is old and who is young
the eyes that told me of the webs they spun
children grow aged over night
when their hula hoops get thrown away
and the old grow to children again
I have found in their eyes
the deliverance of a guttural dream
created again through second birth
this time with subtracted ignorance
added compassion, understanding
full with each moment
and still brave enough to crawl with juicy eyes
the judges that hide fate's fabric
and dampen our warm golden evenings with cold
stand shivering themselves beneath turning old
beneath nature's blue moon
the wolves prowl for soul
She, in the woods running from a fairy tale
and finding what is deep and buried within
She is a bottle of flames that heats amber to stone
not too beautiful to crawl
not too camouflaged to be seen
decorated only by moisture
a cave woman in modern clothes
shadow and light
the yin of her yang
invited in by a separate reality again.

Paragon Space

Neolithic litany chants backwards potency into my lost mind's eye,
paving paragon space for the ultimate embrace
with the I who has traveled the timeless geometric patterns of sound waves,
transmuting the knots of abandoned possibility
into beings with glorious white wings of beginning.

To sanctify home
we pull uncharted lands into our beings
with the found mudras of wizardry
of which re-pattern our future's history
and cleanse the Earth of her incessant bleeding.

because
we
as the only species able to cry salt watered shivers of plea
shatter iron bridges with our earthquakes,
sculpt monsters to life with our pains,
count coins to measure our potency,

We go insane.

Artists make lousy slaves.

November Lament

The smooth bare backs of angels
stretch psalms across seas
that divide our merging
and poison our seeds
Faintly
these
turquoise lullabies
ease homes into this wing fluttered heart
that beats caverns into eyes
and tear oceans of melancholy dreams.

In silent nights,
when we realize
when we realize
the psyche starved debris of enslavement
that has painted our beauty catatonic
and blackmailed our own souls into captivity.

The wounded deer of vulnerability
opens wide the doors of nearly anything
and subconsciously drinks the blood
of this limbo stitched mediocrity.
When we realize
the hungry primal growl of our mass murdering history
disguised as our father
our lord
our victory.

Our mother untouched
ignored beneath the dirt of amnesia,
emerging,
unrecognized
by her beloved children of light.
The light
burrowed beneath pangs of tears
unable to break through the tar of fears.
The light
suffocated by this fatal inability
to see

that god, spirit
everything

is vibrating
Dancing with the serpent of fertility
moving with the grace of tranquility
How perfect is this breath
that speaks to this lucidity

Allow me to express
my ode to the unearthly activated beings
that visit our longings
to rekindle the flame in our minds
that light the dark pathways of our timeless souls

We have curled into fetal lament within this absence of love

It has come so far
we have even forgotten to feel
when the flower of life has withered and died

Ode to the beings of desperate plea
that pray to the all encompassing palms of healing
Ode to the delicate spiders
that are weaving the tattered quilt of consciousness whole again
so that we may sleep sound like children
Ode to the feet with the souls of saints
that carry us in devotion to the river at the top of this mountain
Ode to the long haired maiden that carries the beast with kindness
Ode to the child skipping stones of forgiveness.

Myth Explosion

In one breath
I fell from the tower for 1000 lifetimes
The sound of the unbolted melody of saints
Nearly murdered me with its beauty
For I was barely able to contain
the depth of catharsis that found me
Unbound
The bronze hero of bounty
Drowned her hand in the hearts of many

And chiseled ice sculptures with our sobriety

The mind fills like rain floods entirely
Vigorous man stout and ready
Immeasurable immensity
My heart aches with strings
And buds roses that vibrate at 300 mega hertz
Teaching me how deep elegance can be

Yes to love
And yes to wings

Muscles Grew

A great wind writes me into existence
and swallows me
to become his belly
I chant backwards
litany cleansing my soul
found suddenly
woven by the eons of time
I face this face of mine
captivating the movements of moods
pronouncing my birth given name
not the birth by the brunette song of fire that loved me
but the birth of the dream
by the dew speckled petals that created the thought of me

My muscles never grew from chasing you
the robust thigh bones of the ebony deity that sways inside of me
She just swung in the hammock of my laziness
and yelled celestial obscenities into my once gated matrix
my eyes grew shrewd by watching you
accepting fruit
from the generous baskets of hope you weave
and the calloused stories you tell
ingrained into the crumbling stone tablets at my feet
my heart melted lilac beneath the heat of our merging
drinking fire to ensure my safety

I stood alone at your altar

baptizing the thoughts of a baby
the worlds in my womb
swell and take me
not accepting your last name
roses with thorns of solitude grow around me

though I am breeze bound and wing found
constantly
by the beam downs I pray to for release

My muscles never grew from chasing you
you holy fool who found me
I am seven pointed star
just look at my body.

Me Amour Liaison

Silence calls to me in the form of a feeling
I cannot,
 must not
 ignore this seeing
I would like to be alone with you in our home
to graze the moments of intimacy
that petroglyph the walls of our unity

Love is communion
with the third being
between we

love is the paintbrush
that expresses me

Your body heats
like the core of this pearl
it moves me
like the sanctified holy heart beating
curled inside of your feeling
I am as tiny as a hopeful seed
crowned queen by the prince of nothing
Palm,
 cupping pure bird breathing
The inhalation of hope
 exhaling the fear
and the foggy windowpane of tomorrow
 becoming clear
 rhythmically I shake
 like a glass earthquake
 kneeling before our lady grace
 to know
 that she is holy
 and to fall
into the trusting palms of the infinite being
 is to be washed
 so very clean
that even the obtrusions of mind
 hail to the victory
 that ironically
 is so easy
 as simple as breathing.

Lotus Speech Mandala

The heart ripens robust heat
to be eaten by celestial beings
transmuted to blood
birthing babies with stars for cells
tonight
I learned of God
suddenly struck by its immensity
discovering that there is indeed a gate
that has been built around me
built of the clay of Earth
slowly disintegrating
with its fall
are my own tears of compassionate healing
a warrior's posture with Shambhala crown?
like a spear to the sun
feeling the deep waves of soul finding me
tonight my ego turned to dust
as my body moved in circles
shaping ancestral language on my tongue
my heart leapt
Into an astral lullaby of hope for us
because the vapors of snake
cradling hummingbird
holding air
evoked a deep nostalgia of unity
I am comfortable speaking feelings
with sound
allowing vibrations to heal broken seeds
the Earth pulls me with her density
and ignites me with her flame
A dream: Enable my mind to be like a sky
vast and open
so I may fly.

"Illuminations" by Michael Brown

An Angel's Back

The heart shaped shoulder blades
of an angel's back
pull my eyes to her
into the silent forests of night
a symphony of organic noise
and symbiotic exchange
move me
The Buddha has tilted eyes
towards the underground city
she is holding the golden light like a child
her reflection is a shadow behind her
demolishing identity
overlooking her winged back
geometry is an effortless equation
that makes up the pathways of her mind
She is colored by a new planet's pull

Holding the node of creation in her crown

Jaguar Hummingbird Mantra

Sweeping into your orbit
your gravity helps me rest
peaceful cupped hands
holding birthed child that I am
to drink wisdom in a cup of ancient bliss
soars my wings freely
into unoccupied skies of healing
our galaxy is profound
containing all emotion
and pain
equally shooting stars of fire
and ice
into souls that breathe rain

Coiling serpent with scarab eyes
twists
like DNA inside of me
shaping patterns of sound
dreams and words
upon lips that see me
ego sliced in salvation
I return home

I must learn to turn
gold into radioactive saliva
to lick
the gates that bind me away
to make love to my enemies
is to beckon them into spheres of eternal bliss
with love alone
I must do this

War is a forceable vile energy
that wears masks
of resolve
disintegrating masks

you find megalithic lullaby
to bring home to me
reeking of fearless space
and otherworldly epiphanies
making home as turtle's backs
we bring our temples with us

God bless the souls who
long to transform into higher realms
peace soaking into hearts
feeding universal order
and celestial tongue

May spirit's vast creation become us

Holy maidens of prayer
and purge

Respect the process of zero
and silence
wed to eternity
I wear gold petaled honor of your melting

Universe
weeping eons of tears
suppressed
arms stoicly holding
blue pearl in anguish
sculpting peace statues
for freedom's sake
coded in my blood
is ancestral DNA

Deeply crusted jewels of Earth
helps me remember my mother
VIVA to our mothers!

My mother
is fierce delicacy
forever holding me
she is scent sweet
and birthed me

from a seed
I grew inside of her belly
drinking her joy

and tears

My great mother is holy crested soil
of amythest and jade
holding all memories of all souls
she perpetually births me

In fetal curl
one can swirl entirely into vast black space
rhythmically gestating with solar feeling

let her weep
let her weep
let this fair child free
burdens of planets weep in our hearts
we cry purification waters
alleviating imprisoned minds

exhale deep scar tissue
into mamma's rich soil

when I learn to think with my feelings
I can listen to the cellular memories of my soul

Global Warning

Sometimes,
When the miracle of life is suddenly forgotten
If ever I feel that this thread is my last
this imperative link
that weaves me to god
If ever its extinction seems possible
then I have been taken like a porcelain puppet by fear
This illusion,
(That this braid
to this god
is not woven
with my DNA itself
or that my every thought
is not so tenderly touched
by the prophetic palms of angels
or that each moment is not a chance to glide again
upon spirit's silvered beckoning)
This illusion,
is the genocide of love
When I must muster up every fiber of courage in me
just to remember
that this body
is a temple
in which great beings of light
conceive...
When the world,
painted like a surreal concept,
churns my stomach
with its opaque concrete ideas
and its amphibious lust for pain
Its inability to say....
"please.....somebody... Help me know love"
When the bitter cravings of mankind consume beauty
leaving nuclear dust trails as foot-prints
upon the ice covered earth
When I realize this is a part of me
When it all seems like a dark, impossible dream
Please,
Somebody,
Wake me.
there are so many vagabonds searching for the soul
that deep and bottomless place
lined with the magic of snake

that eats our withered tears
and recycles our fathered fears
This holy place in the dark
we are too afraid to venture into alone
because the vastness
and the unknowable
terrifies our minds
shatters our falsified image of self
or togetherness
I'll tell you what togetherness is
what NOT being alone IS
it is the union of compassion
For this temple called earth
(our body)
She is in need of our love
and we project that need as our own
but cover it in a mask as fear of rejection
this really IS happening
hearts are becoming cold
in the furious loss of light
we've stripped the sun of her god-woven coat
now, she burns naked
melting our ice
flooding our earth
meanwhile, war.
we kill each other
because of fear
because we cannot find our spirit's voice
My heart is now pounding
for the safety of our children
Suddenly...
the convenience of tupperware
doesn't seem worth it
The brilliance of industry
seems like a bloodthirsty weapon
re-producing itself in armies of Wall-Marts
oil has been bartered for precious blood
brown blood
the color of this earth
why do we kill
the color of this earth?
there are angels here to help
and you are one of them
this is not being alone
this is compassion in unity.

Grandmother's Seam

The immensity of light
is so profound
that I wept for an eternity before it

This utterly solid snake

not from beyond
but here within my very own core

I love thee
I honor thee
I kneel before thee in prayer

knowing nothing else to do in your divine presence
other than deeply bow

So entirely eternal I am created of thee
the infinite source we call God
we call medicine

we call to in our dreams with our soul's lucid voice
is so small
I have no human name for you
my gifts are wept through my eyes to you
grounded root of birth
exquisite artist of eyes
may I be born into your light?
absorbed of you
so that I may bring you as a message of light to my brothers and sisters

Take me back before time equated my path with symbols and mind

Take me back before I shook like a rhythmic gentle earthquake when touched

We all come to you someday

You
who has been visited by fleets of angels
your depth is but a fraction of your vast ocean
I am levitating in cocoon
that transforms us all
I am not I at all
but we
breathing along to the same gentle frequency

My soul is taught how to pray
so that the Earth may be at peace

Ever Spiraling

When i reach out to the palms of blackness
and clutch her charcoaled ash toned fingertips
Watch
as the multitudes of mind clouds disperse
For her sight
that ruthless light that heals the blind
is just so bright
that you might find your soul reflected in its fury

Do not be drunk by this wild inquisitive lover of mind
when i reach into the palms of space
to pull this psychic conversation into form

i am awakened
by the freedom of our touch
and like the leaves
that paint themselves like fingertips upon my eyelashes of gold
i tumble between time, timelessness, spaciousness and the cracks between
the window sills
i am the caterpillar
the moth
the butterfly
the cocoon
and the creator that painted the picture
within this ecosphere
i am just a sphere
spiraled into myself vibrantly
like whirling dervish
I am curled

Dirty Megalithic Space

In guiltless celebration
i am raptured by what is true
As I watch the refined colorful women
squirming in dirt
eating rainbows
escaping this subterranean eon of neon knives
and whisking their tail-feathers into space
metagalactic space...
the vacuum that eats our coiled strife
and uncoils it back to love.
we dance
to release the poetry
but when the collide of fireworks in our eyes is reduced
to a Hollywood pizzazz
tragedy consumes the ethers
and when we are curling ourselves into our own hearts
exploding like lava
into each other's souls
we are each like the pearl in the dirty clam's mouth of miracles
The awakened hearts are sailing on shattered pieces of Earth
holding wide eyes against gravity

i heard a story
of a man who sailed past 10 days of not talking
sitting
just breathing
like he
I am in the woods
and silent
bridging the dive into the core
Rewiring the matrix of thought
There are no limitations to the self
no routines to the soul
no boxes in the macrocosmic drop
he breaks the box into space
and it evaporates

becomes the stardust we used to be
and invites me to a tea party
cradle space
and soothe moon gazes upon my back behind me
The new sight beyond dusty nights
every word is breathing stones
thick air evaporates in smoke
as we dry our insides from wet
I saw love before there were words to define its mood
The gasping air
catapulting in my throat
I tune my world to ballerina feet
I am opened carefully
seeds trailing home behind me
If you crave beauty
in all of its bounteous buoyancy
then come with me
witness pyramids as foreheads
looking into the sky
i am not shy
i am not shy

Day of Flight

I do not yearn today for anything.
I do not bind myself echo machine
to your marriage vows of isolation
I am not the caterpillar denied access to wings
I cannot jump fast enough from this dimension I have landed upon
to satisfy my people of poetic perfection.
This unspeakable mood of simplicity just is
I am
I am the archetypal wing into mystery of which my long bird-like neck cannot see
I have suffered the in-between
lost between serious victory
this is my last time here
I understand the underneath
first, the truth of mystery
the piece by piece puzzle that was smashed
and thrown to the hungry fire wrath
This is free
This is seed
this is the infinite drop into eternity
that embellished itself before the king
with whispers for vocal cords
and dew drops for hands
slightly outrageous with a mad-man's scream
uncovered by the curious eyes of innocent dreams
I was picked like a flower's stem in the cave of never never land
there were finally trees uncut and unafraid to speak to me
Finally, the deep sea has invited me
Quartz bottoms of my crystal ocean
here where I did not hide to sing
cuddled the vast oceans ethereal hush
as The sky falls blue damp tear forms into the child's palm
It is wrapped around my blue neck
and massaging mangos into my throat
I am again on earth
as servant to the grace
and watcher of tarantulan fire
crawling shyly in the corner of my eye
This breath I have breathed since freedom was free
was the starlight map of our divinity
A forgotten dance has moved into me
It moves me to merge with this gliding galaxy
Now is the movement of our infinity
as passers of the circus stare daydreaming

"Seeing Through the Patterns" by Michael Brown

Crossbone God

The brilliance of creation
Pumps
Ionic mystery into my veins
sprouting
a deep desire
to love
with each cell
that vibrates in this nebula of conception
I am part of a divine family
an ageless clan
our blood flows as a river's might
into the unlimited ocean of life
not the blood of stigmata
but the blood of re-creation
the blood of miracles
to birth prayer
to birth the ancient voices of our future
we cry god's tears
though we are not disciples in your church
we steep stronger
in gods serum of truth
though we are not silent nuns in your monastery
We are children of god's temple
beings of holy light
though we are not the pure sacrifice
on your iron cross of shame
she and he
conceived within the desire of a dream
witnessed beneath Gods holy microscope
Illusion slain by the immaculate spear
awakened to the worlds of wisdom beneath our skins
who is this God?
It is beyond the linear thinking of who
It is essence
that bends gracefully around the mind
Revealed poetically in scents of Sanskrit and lime
It is effortless
thoughtless
unable to be contemplated

for its size
its shape
is beyond the metric system
deeper than love can be barely tasted
God is written in beautiful letters
spoken in a language of shivers
I feel this vibration
this beautiful blue electricity
bolting like lightning in my heart
I am utterly in love
with this concept of God
this holy place I have known
since timelessness struck my soul
allow us to love this god
without the aid of a story
without the guilt of shame
for we
are forever woven
to a sacred feeling
of which god has braided us into
so for the sake of our children
un-grip us psychically
we are levitating
in the hands of love
while vibrating in peace
outside of your iron church doors of chastity
where we have sailed the infinite dream
before metal was melded into a cross
before man
sunk his sacrificial stone
into the weightlessness of freedom
Allow us to be completely undone
by the utter mystery of this journey
with no final answers to obstruct our searching
with no box to contain our receptivity
far beyond this collective scream to be loved
and far past our history of ravished blood
We are free
We are alive in every cell of our beings
We are free
We are free
We are free_

Collage of Fate

In my rose quartz heart
that bleeds the blood of hummingbird love
I fit with you
as though you were puzzle
and I am piece
This essence that proclaims itself as you
so gently carves itself into my bones
Not as forgotten atmosphere might merge
abrubtly
but already
your rhythm is my sound
the song that carries
the voice that hears
Here in this layered pavilion
of emotionally armed lovers
the watchers
the saints
the inbetween calls me
birthing my uncaged wings to life
restoring my delicate frequency
carrying me home
to the spacious face

I savor the mangos on your lips
I am a collage of fate

Love Poem to a Clown

magnetically pulled into your view
morphing into your muse
beside the glimpse of your punch line
carved into this back to back mediation
a curiosity rapidly breathes in me
watcher of the movements between
where the dance is cradled by your fragrance
un lost
but wandering
this labyrinth sinks its walls

Holy Spirit Comforter

We are wrapped in the cocoon of this mortal womb
while landslides of time
dilute our potency
We slice open the sky
to unveil what we may see
only to be fooled by another mystery
Vagabond, Healer, Child,
If you are to dance in the acid rain today,
in a sleepless
dreamless
daze
with your demise amplified
and your colorblind skies
I will pray for your new eyes
because to be asleep in this decadent dream
is like the devil killing Eve
Though,
I am not beside myself in grief
I let the boogy-man go long ago
he no longer haunts my eyes of belief
for I have the skeleton key of joy in my breath
the rhythmic trance of love in my chest
See, It's this Godly touch of fire fingers
that dries my eyes of tears
a bell that rings nostalgic memories
of a Holy Spirit comforter
wrapping me into sleep.
this has burned inside this ivory soul
this forgiven freedom
this mind
as friend
as sight
as creator
as light
Gather within this Earthly sphere
to speak galactic linguistics.
hold this heart near.
refuse the poisoned drink
of tomorrow's fear.

Holy Spirit Comforter,
we are alive!
breathing the sounds of the soul's chimes!
It is so soul train, you and I.
Woman,
if you have lost your reflection,
look firmly into the deep
See the eye
the Eye that drips of golden epiphany
when you make love
make love with the Gods of eternity
with my wandering swift feet
can you live with me so free?
will you wander back to sleep?
In a daze
of a laser eyed
petrified
candied maze?
where the holy spirit comforter
Cannot hold you in her sheets?
because you have lost the secret to keep
Can you live alive?
Awake?
and free?
Though I am a dream
dreamed of by me
and you are too
and now we can't tell who's who
We are moving by the whim of water
like rebellious salmon upstream
with delicately woven wings
like canary queens giving birth
to the effervescent in-between
Here, In this wind tunnel of shape
I have found sharp sliding snakes
hunting for a soft cry
while listening to the harp
stream feeding sounds from our sky
moving me into this body
where I am the feeling of she
rowing in this soul
searching in this sea

stillness is the door
curiosity, the key.
She...the roped into earth Queen
buried in the sands of Pixie
shouting
"We are ALL family!"
in this cold underground of Persephone
it is cold soil indeed
but deep
It's the song that reminds you
"You DO hold keys!"
It is not sorrow
or pain
or misery
It's divine banshee wine
being drunk by eternity
screaming from space
"I am a seed!"
God has burrowed a hole like a bear
and is hibernating within your skin
so cast away this stone in you
and release the pent up scream
cackle like Genie
that's escaped from the lamp
Be your own master!
Be in your own trance!
if you wish to be reborn as bat
to move so fast
to seed the souls of love in its path
to be the weird poetry
of the dancing bee
while planted in the soil
it is cold indeed
but deep

God Sings in Her Voice

There is a muse of rapture within me
with claws growing to the point of pyramids
moving her way through my density
turning my blood
to a dark shade of release
she chants her way to my attraction
and perches on the edge of my balance

calling to the lives of the past
the bodies she knew as mine
to shed wings and fly from their pains
I am her midwife
preparing my own womb for the explosion
of she
birthed into being
I carry the weight of her screams
My solemn eyes cry tears for sanity

She holds the love we could ripen to be
in the ways she boldly spreads her wings

In her absence
I have cried the river
that she has become fish and glides within

She rattles my soul to sing her name
ISIS
mother of mothers
I crave to combust
into a million pieces of her essence
so that she may fall
like snow
upon each vital creature
that breathes

I pray for this masterpiece
I lay awake in this epiphany
covered in white flag
I've declared peace in my sleep
and died at the feet of this war's fantasy
When, my friends of velvet Eden
may we inhale this new beginning?
the clock is ticking

the revolution is screaming
the crone is burning

Chastise me
condemn me
burn me at your stake of fear
and misery
for believing
for loving
for midwifing beauty
for dreaming
for seeing
for becoming a part of your history

but i am not your enemy

I am the snake
with a spine of iron thorns
that kills your purgatory

I am a palette for spirit's eternal song
I am the ground you walk upon
I am the voice in your head
that longs to be free

a mindless heartbeat
the river's silent poetry

I am before the yin and the yang
were forbidden to merge
I am the dot
on the saddhus forehead
that leads you back to zero
I am the you
that knows she is me

I am the woman
burned at the stake for believing
for loving
for midwifing beauty
the parts of history
you don't read
the secret part of humanity
emerging from the cracks of infinity

to redefine reality

Earth Crone

That sweet succulence of rose
This came from our Earth
This delicacy of pink petal eyes
Awake to the Northern sky
This is our Earth
Roots curling themselves between one another
Ancient and woven to our very veins that breathe her name
This grace of touch
The softness of pale fingertips
This is a reflection of our divine mother that cradles our labrynth minds
And ignites the light to love again
This- this perfection is our gracious mother
Ever forgiving of her wild banshee children
I smile to watch her as I weep
For her immensity of love is shocking
I vibrate in kundalini knowing before her golden light
I am so happy to be with her upon her body
May I be of service to help heal you?
As you have healed me
Though I am so small and you are everything
All ignited in life force
Generous enough to pass through my being
Cleansing me of that
which keeps me from you

Crawling to Eden With a Smile

This ancient scroll i unroll again
to drink the days when there was then
articulate wrists daydreaming of a dream
where she can finally sing soul's song
a candle light heart to light the dim room
a wind chime mind
i set sail to the deep blue void
there are no footsteps behind me
hiding my masks from my heart's honesty
and sound in the palms that heat around me
in this existence
we are truth beneath the uniform
and long deeply to be unveiled
like gypsy runaways to Eden
before the diamond light turned pale
sedated by mythological monsters
half asleep
and half panicked
as mimes to our feelings
we drown
in the slumber of this needing
camoflauged by the suns bleeding light
if our senses are to deprive themselves of sight
then We are in need of some kind of godly wind
some kind of inspiring song that sings us into bliss
awake us to this thunder!
cover us in nectar
teach us to play
slip us the potion
feed us the way

Infant Superhero

I parachute from space
into your arms like tektite amber
bringing the message of wordless song
from a telepathic nation
a purple planet
a cranial explosion
eyes teared
no illness
palms wrinkled
soft
a sun or two
blazing growth of green
to reshape our sculpture
falling obese like melting sap upon dying trees
to re-calculate our equation
from a negative mistake
to a multiplied spade
to weave the branch back
where the bow broke
to cradle our infancy
in velvet cloaks
fuschia light in the eyes of all we know
i bring the soil of life to help us grow
We are so full with the ions of soul
and yet we bury ourselves like the hunted mole
I come from a purple planet
of the modern antique doll
already shattered by the cataclysm of thought
rebuilt
re-seeded
re-inspired
by love
vibrant as the fires raised eyebrow
gentle as the rivers silken dance

we are gamblers
coral coal miners
ruthless daisy bomb droppers
reality hoppers
blue flame hypnotists
galaxy operators asking for directions
bowing to peace
levitating in the in-between
wondering who will see

A Caterpillar's Reality

canary feathers in pale orange light
spread across my spine in flight
like my hearts open shark mouth bite
in this microscopic time-line
imagining me from the inside
to your hungry animal thighs
i may as well be served on ice
like faucet leaks and angel wings
and tadpoles that sing to me
my hat is off to the dingbat
that remembers to laugh at me
and the hunter that flies in the crimson night
his cleft chin dreams of red apocalypse
washed upon the sandy ocean beach
not chained anymore are my dreams
I've found the key
sleeping inside of an opal's fairy ring
madrone is my favorite tree
like tantric tumbling feet
pounding footsteps into earth
imprinting the big bang sonic boom into existence
When these elongated moments evaporate
and this image I hold of she
disintegrates
the smoke rings
and the hypnotized snakes of grace
calls to me
i dive in decadently
into the spring of water's touch
scarcely fingering fire long enough to drink her burn
transforming the seed of this belly that bleeds
stones shape themselves in halves
and wholes
puppet shows
electric glows
honey wine
this is my shrine

this is why
i fall so
deeply
into those glowing eyes
This free falling into the castles hush
softly with this sheer tongue
transparent to the days
that blinded me with sun rays
phoenix winged
reborn from seed
unable to be contained
expanded into the rain
drops become my name
rounded to sharp
to rounded again
this is the friend
crawling out from within
shading the light caves with dim
catching my empathy tears in a thimble
I use to sew my life back together
into a warm seamless blanket of seeds
the mirror's shape-shifting gaze
speaks to my inner mind with ease
of space eyes cast in green
like the dreamed prairies roaming through me
to be beyond obscene
to slide in between
as THIS unravels the stitch of my seams
willingly
this
has reached the corest core of my being
it continues onward
to a dense infinity
intertwined with the picture framed memories of history
perhaps i am just the fractal imagery
pigments of what i think they see in me
and to whirl out by chance
these gentle hurricanes
and into you
to subjectively view
this full form
which even to me is new.

Lucid Migrant

Sunday is flooding
ice caps of madness
as the newborn weeps
ameythest tears of heat
dreaming in her sleep
of our ancient grandmother
with beautifully withered hands and feet

she reminds her of ancient hypothesis
a catalyst of metamorphosis
so that the spirit may again soar free
through the white crystallized droplet of mind
Mountain caps
familiar white
paint dreams of life

I awake
struck by the starkness of night
wings mended by the simple meditation
braided entirely to the holy sacrum
The newborn heats under the sun
of a hundred piercing eyes
as fear subsides
she finds grace and kindness
in the deities trance
struck by the holy song of this eternal moment
Water turns to smoke
when fire finds it
hypnotizes minds free
as I search for a tree to sleep beneath
even the clouds cover me
even the sea bathes me
transmuting the carbon of modern life extremity
to lime green power guided by the rains purity
exposing
the innocence of love
and the unveiled face
I've touched by taste in this dream

S.O.S

Flowers are hungry for pure oxygen
they wilt in tar
they sing in air
as she pierces with her golden eye
she spins her web stoicly
and dances in her cloak of fire
like some mad dervish spider
the ticking clock silences
like the tantric yes to life
able to endure all sight
slicing the thick smog of smoke
into bittersweet honesty
i dive in decadently

Red Window

I am a phantom to myself
Thus sculpting my pen as a paintbrush when you sing to me in rhyme
Shaping sound machines to lullaby's
Soothing the mind's chafed eyes
Red cape fire winged wyvern listening
Cupping wind like wounded child
Mother soul imprinted history
Carries me through moonless nights
To the deities of flight, my head is a shaven alter of surrender
Offering womb water to mouths that thirst

Sleeping in Rhythm

In this bedroom
my fingertips paint the opaque walls bright
and the vital needs of my inner song to be sung
is as alive as the cradled doll in a little girl's mind
I am observing the shadow of candle light dreams
soaring into you
then soaring into me
It is of a cryptic code
that I did break
while gazing
into the cast eyes of our eternity
I did not fade away
into this tender and poetic day

I have embodied the woman of boundless energy
by frequenting the thoughts of exquisite beauty
beside every crevice of fractal fertility
I am seen by your dream
I am shattered by its scream
I am lost in a paradise of bliss
as I claw into your delicate back again
The thorn in my side that allowed me to hide
has softened to a round gem
It is glowing in the face of our freedom
and singing of a forgotten song to mend

This is the band of the flying phoenix
released from the quickening sand
spread open at last
glowing in the gaps
between the known and unknown lands of woman

In The Heat Of Texas

while sleeping on the concrete in your withered barn
bones take shape to a lion's mane
backward yard dog delight
tracing the shapes of the sky
this moment of planetary shift
happens in my soul again
amidst the wood's drift
and the river's silken kiss
awake i pray
for our mother to be unslaved
today i say
these lines in tongue
to your heart unstrung
multitudes of faces change
i cry beside your calling
you and I
are not so delicate
we are solid earth
together we merge
our bottomless feet
from space we are levitating
shaking

"Cerebrellation" by Luke Brown

A Rare Dream

white elephant with plants of trees for hair
shades indigo with lilac blood rare
upon blank canvas screaming to sing
amplified love am I
before this golden dream
rooted limbs are mine
while thunderous secrets whisper seeds
I clasp palms to prayer
within your eccentric sphere of rest
and limbo levitating dualities

that merge to sleep on your breast

Airport

airport women
gazing into the hypnosis of channel nine's
benign sleep
sit next to Shamu the caged whale
eating krispy kream donuts
not noticing the smog

i sit stoic in pink lace
cramped womb
focusing my inner guru
upon disintegrating the glued glass
that cages the free

Black Crow Embryo

My embryonic alter ego
reaches to taste recognition

But I step back
into warm void palms that cradle this infancy
prowling proud lioness mother awake
to a lucid dream of life

Saints don't look away from blood
and daze into distant turquoise mindscape
escaping from nothing
to go nowhere

gently becoming air
breath from each pore that drinks orgasmic light alive

last meal chewed thoroughly
black crow circling

On this alchemical jungle trail into light rays
comets birth milk maidens
with rose petaled fingertips
un-doing done deals of massacre
unfreezing stories upon silent lips

The last tree grows stoic and firm
budding babies blossoming with birth

through the iron stapled hunt of the hungry
dreaming the dark tender underbelly
of what we've yet to see

Medicinally, I eat the seed that showers me
and wash it down with the light of infinity
to move mountains meticulously
we build homes in the spaces between we
turning nightingale songs into prescriptions
laying swords to sleep
upon white feathered bed's of beauty

Originally,
we are made of this
climactic time capsule of now
of which we all breathe life into being

resurrecting the death of lament

Sinking into a songbird's memory
of being air
we explode empty
to feel liberated from gravity

as we are beside she

when my mother sleeps deep
I dream

My sister speaks effervescent obscurity
fluently
to the rarest parts of my being
the parts born in this moment
of fragmented blossoms
blowing rhythmically
to the sound of pure hearts meeting
I stand
barely formed
before the greatest artist unborn
cloaked in a slippery liquid
you can't hold onto
this is truth
raw pink
and shallow
and deep
with no pattern to cut into

Breathe Earth Breathe

Milky moments notoriously sour
spoiling perfect air to space
I am on display as person
for space to be defined
and picked apart
until cells become so heavy with judgment
that they wither in health and vitality
I am beyond labeling of emotional captivity
and find resonance in simply being
void of color swabs to taste test my personality
melting into a prayer I spoke on my higher behalf
to see faces morph to moods
and swept by caressing recognition
bridges form in my heart
to my mind's jewel bodied chrysalis
that holds sacred my silence
and womb water like warmth
Even as melodic as the symphony please
lay awake in dreams I am a lucid sea
baked in the heart of a mother is free
wound tight to be released rhythmically
i hold shian mudra pose
with the earth breathing beneath me

River Dream

You fall from my lips like vintage wine
staining my heart in red memory
vivifying the liquid moth meditating inside of me
star gazed and tame
You are perfectly ripe
with silence sleeping in your eyes
as deep as a birds need to fly
In this waiting for you
I have found a most spacious craving
portrayed a most ancient being
sustained a most limitless feeling
satisfied by this nostalgia of seeing
A simple gaze comes through
I step inside of you
To view my galaxy through binoculars of new
drinking your delicate night shaded mead
intoxicated by the need
I have this dream:
the coyote of antiquity chases the smell of your lucidity
I whistle to distract the carnal destruction
man falls to his knees
teeth sharpen as tongue licks corners of desire
I am a warrior of no weapons
no white flag
You are light itself
blinding me brilliantly
Finally we bask in the beauty of not seeing
I am the seed of your children's sleep
barely blending into my surroundings
I drink laughter
By way
Of the
Clowns
spoon feeding me
I also drink tea
Combined with infinity
Dust in my eyes
Crossing the road before me
I am as dense as gravity

As loose as the river's tranquility
Softened to cloud essence
by the love of your epiphany
rounded to a circular geometry
I come upon a little river
A little shotgun madness reminds of yesterday
When I lived on the other side of the swamp's misery
the tired side of the ever changing eternity
exploding beneath the shadows of the sun
the gaze of god rendering me undone
and now,
becoming this complete sound
this entirely merged existence of ONE
Love,
collaborating in rhythm to my heart's beat
My selves,
racing each other into this perfect state of beauty

Scribe

Mystic Scribe bathed in regal light
moved by the most high
her voice comes in subtle waves
of whispers between and beyond what we know as time
my heart beats poetry in the walls of your temple
draped in white and pale colors
as subtle as this piece of soul that cradles home

She bathes me in silk
pulling strings of debris down
into the void of soundless frequency
refurbishing my identity
I come to you clean
purified by the form woven sense of my own divinity

I am like you
infused with particles of perfect snow
wet as the birth of a baby
known by ancient deities
that shape star messages
in the forms of feelings inside of she
I go
forest bound
to hear your calling of the cobra
that awakens inside of the seed
with ruby eyes
she is my disguise
beside her, I am pure pink petals in glass casing
untouched by the human parts of me

This is for everyone
this stone etched declaration of love
this essence of original blood

Rest, my mother of marrow
watch the fire dance to the silence
when there is no silence

Feel the spaces of light inflate
between the new bones our skeletons are receiving
Within the new sight our infant race is creating
can you hear god's heart beating?

In Preparation of an Epiphany

Maiden intelligence burns sulphur
to discern waste from sage
It's enticing to bend time
beyond mankind's beast
morphing calloused bygones
to ecstatic dreams
contemplate
the ripeness of
your flowering minds
self-mastery
very soon your molecules
will be in prayer with all that is

Do you know this to be true?
that a birth is coming

Elohim

This crescent etched ember of ash
has fallen from the flame that
soothed my lament
to sleep
In prayer lit rooms draped in violet rays
from eyes that soothe

gaze completely upon my naked being
shaping Elohim into mysterious sound frequencies
taming the savage heat of our separation
into round puzzled pieces that fit
like the cupped hands of
lovers

[this could be the pillaged
prayer my church has
over spoken
branding angles
with archetypes fixed
as sculptures]

I came upon a state
as stone shaped as the surreal fraction
of my being
warmed only by the suns eclipse
found
picked up & treasured
by the holy

I am You

God's eyes are mine
I am the ocean's breath
the light of creation
has made me
My blood is poetry

God has painted me alive
with his voice which speaks
through me
The night sky
whispers incantations of bittersweet
change into my open heart
like you...
I am an ancient
language spoken by few
I recall every child I have
ever birthed and hold their
essence as my truth
Sending love to my son who is
now my brother
letting go of old disguises
created out of terror
fresh naked eyes
are not color blind to this
new vibration of feeling
I cannot
hide
Amethyst birds of prayer
fly out of my throat and
create home in the name
my mother has gifted me
Let this life be nothing but poetry

let me bathe in rich soil and
cleanse my heart in the
depth of your tone
Coursing fire through my veins which
is tamed by the weightlessness
of water
Merged
Woven and
symmetrically spoken
our souls
fade into brilliant Gold
beside the sounds of dakini's dancing
every graceful foot paving
passageways home

Key

I see myself in your gaze
below the breath of the Earth that fills me
the breath that nourishes
the harmonic pasture of my potency
Your kisses cleanse the
martyr out of me
brewing with the beat of my soul's
thesis
the neophyte footsteps of my ascension
pearls of pineal plasma
you gift to me
making temples out of catastrophes
the gentle nuances
of your movement sets
caged birds free
from the vocal box that speaks for me
I see myself in your perception
Dreaming cocoon like
in your gossamer
my iridium iris
awake to our flame

Cyclone Banshee

The taste of my fear is bitter
and the sound of my flesh
against flesh
that does not match
my hidden form
is a sharp ringing
an undeniable banshee singing
I am a vortex infused cyclone to you
as though my skin
is not soft & warm as a mother
pheasant's wing
for centuries
I have been licking myself clean

but the pollutants of
man's apathy breeds silver life
into every crevice
as I fall into pieces
helpless
before the dominion of
cyclical skyscrapers dotting
permanent I's
contracts
that steal life
these are my prayers
in tandem with this wild decay
this is my lord Shiva
ripping the heads off of
small pigeons to resurrect them
coursing rainwater through
hungry veins
knitting velvet
upon a lonely face

You are the archaic
madness

stoic stone collapse

Your feet
are the rusted anchors
that implanted themselves
from flight
the possible surrender of your
fight births a hopeful
imagination to my
judgemental rage
carving passageways home
my soul had forgotten
I cradle the future on my
hand woven rug that houses
a temple for fire
to lean life into me
My eyes are thirsty
I think I only have two
friends
really
two who wouldn't
hold me from a state of
falling
but fly down into
the tunnel with me to
accompany my frailty
I am not imaginary
of pretending to be queen
but I am a tiny piece of
everything
paradoxically coupled
with this eternal identity.

Diamond Soul

How Many lines have been spent
connecting to my beloveds through
the pen?
Rotations move
the mountains beneath me
so my journey is not so
arduous
and memories...
liminal in their form move through me,
collaging the pieces of my
puzzling mind into sacred shape
enough to witness the
raw diamond center of soul
that weeps & laughs
simultaneously beckoning
the birth of its singularity
which is summoned smaller
than molecular form
until it explodes at once
into everything
fueling the
angel's epiphany of itself
by merely humbling
itself into courageously
becoming one single dot.
this is the honesty of
existence
wrathful
and raw
and perfect.

Between Breath

Between your lips
is the curve of prophetic poetry
beckoning
me into being

in full form I
shift and sway
to this storm
curling chaos of sound waves
with my
tongue's wet landscape

upon raw bare bone altars
lay
poignantly chosen stones
to
geometrically lay the patterns
of my home into

where I float into absent gravity

where my translucent
mother
holds my heavy
head
with her soft
rose petaled agony

Bold Heros

I sell my words
I move my hips

I shift my eyes to watch you slip
into rabbit's holes of no return
where owls hide & trick you with
soft lullabies

Heroes are bold
gold in the spectrum of the rainbow
looking you dead on in the eyes
to say "I love you"
as though there were no past

I thrive with dirt in my eyes
carrying the candle's light
beside the sound of your tone
you
whom I refer to as he
no need for a name
beside this woven web
you have strung to my soul
he is solid amethyst light
the highest thought from above
that sees through the hawk eyes gaze
a yellow solid wing span
protecting shoulders blades of
glass
I am a wonderland
of taste
only cultured
souls can sink into

let me curl time before you

to find prophetic cave bound
offerings beneath this last
standing tree
though each
moment may seem long
they are fleeting
and looked back upon with elongated hearts
remembering the depth of the
cave we stumbled within
as only
a memory
a birth
born of death.

In this Night

This is the first thought of existence
exploding itself into form
Unaware of its own reflection
other than that that is everything
and this is the first realization of singularity
where the pressure of form has contained itself into one single point
beside this ember trenched oasis
for ice to become air

In what form do you entice the calling?

You are the molecules in everything
expressing itself in maladies and whispers
the vibration between your feet and the soil is rich
and when they touch
the unity of two unlikely lovers is celebrated

Newborn essence speaks in rhythm

If you catch a wave upon the swooping saliva of a first breath
carried in and witnessed by the barely breathing
bring the light into your decension
remind us that calcified stones are breakable
and that archaic truth does not die

This birth
is like the sudden pop of newfound energy
It's like when you suddenly observe
the timelessness of your own love

You suddenly witness the depth of your abyss
and you might wonder
"Will you protect me?"

When I am out there
molded as night to the precipitating void?

Will you recognize me?
as I become warped and contorted to the shape of humanity?

Will you follow me into the endless moment?
where we must tame the pillaging fire to simple flame?
where is the ritual of your own salvation?
that greets your eyes to the soil's world?

Whose mother bird are you cupping?
entranced by her beauty but breaking her wings

I have met snakes with rose petals for scales
and I have watched them change form into night

So when you wash me with the snow of water
let the baptism be known

It comes in the form of softer steps
and sharper swords

Listen to the spaces between their words
where you may see the spirit of your essence
peering through to pray with you

About the Author

Taylor Maiden Space is a linguistic seamstress weaving together new patterns of thoughts for all to ponder. A wordsmith compounding the ionic metals of separate realities together to create sculptures of sound and visual imagery. She left high school at 16 to explore the school of bittersweet life experience. At 18 she moved into her cozy 1967 Chevy Van and fled across the country scribbling urgent poetry upon napkins and selling hand made bell-bottoms for money. Thus far, Taylor has explored humanity thoroughly, always observant of the nuances of her surroundings, allowing all to be teachers, hunting for the meaning in between the lines of known reality. She has danced within many different crowds of people, seeking further understanding of her existence. She hungers for knowledge, studies esoteric texts for fun, her heartbeats with Earth's rhythm and ceases with her cries. Taylor is here to assist in the healing of this planet and the ascension of humanity so that we may rise into the light of our true vibrations. Feeling continuously as though Earth is accelerating consciousness at undeniable speeds, she continues to search her soul for new ways to express the strange inner world of her being and swells with cathartic jubilance at the sight of discovered freedom. Her hope is to create a unique reflection of you in her words through the creative subsistence of her existence.

128

www.ingramcontent.com/pod-product-compliance
Lightning Source LLC
Chambersburg PA
CBHW041158290426
44109CB00002B/56